George Washington

By Jevon Bolden

Children's Press®

An Imprint of Scholastic Inc.

Content Consultant
Mary V. Thompson, Research Historian, George Washington's Mount Vernon

Library of Congress Cataloging-in-Publication Data
Names: Bolden, Jevon, author.
Title: George Washington: first president of the United States/Jevon Bolden.
Other titles: First president of the United States
Description: New York: Children's Press, an imprint of Scholastic Inc., 2021. | Series: Presidential biographies | Includes index. | Audience: Ages 7–9. | Audience: Grades 2–3. | Summary: "Book introduces the reader to George Washington and his life." —Provided by publisher.
Identifiers: LCCN 2020002640 | ISBN 9780531130957 (library binding) | ISBN 9780531130674 (paperback)
Subjects: LCSH: Washington, George, 1732–1799—Juvenile literature. | Presidents—United States—Biography—Juvenile literature. | United States—History—Revolution, 1775–1783—Juvenile literature. | United States—History—1783–1815—Juvenile literature.
Classification: LCC E312.66 .B64 2021 | DDC 973.4/1092 [B]—dc23
LC record available at https://lccn.loc.gov/2020002640

Initial Prototype Design by Anna Tunick Tabachnik
Produced by Spooky Cheetah Press
Design by Kimberly Shake

Printed in North Mankato, MN, USA 113

1 2 3 4 5 6 7 8 9 10 R 30 29 28 27 26 25 24 23 22 21

Scholastic Inc., 557 Broadway, New York, NY 10012.

Photos ©: cover, spine, back cover: Superstock, Inc.; 5: Bridgeman Images; 6: Sarin Images/The Granger Collection; 7: Bridgeman Images; 9: Everett Collection Inc/age fotostock; 10: Bridgeman Images; 13: Look and Learn/Bridgeman Images; 14: Superstock, Inc.; 15: Courtesy of the College of Liberal Arts/University of Massachusetts Boston; 16: Superstock, Inc.; 19: Look and Learn/Bridgeman Images; 20: Sarin Images/The Granger Collection; 22: Bridgeman Images; 24: History Archive/UIG/Bridgeman Images; 26: The Granger Collection; 28 tree: Shendart/Getty Images; 30 top left: Superstock, Inc.; 30 top right: The Print Collector/age fotostock; 30 bottom center: Everett Collection Inc/age fotostock; 30 bottom right: Bridgeman Images; 31 top left: Look and Learn/Bridgeman Images; 31 top center: Superstock, Inc.; 31 bottom left: Superstock, Inc.; 31 bottom right: The Granger Collection. All other photos © Shutterstock.

SOURCE NOTES: Page 5: Letter to George Steptoe Washington, accessed at https://founders.archives.gov/documents/Washington/05-07-02-0017; page 9: Letter to Benedict Arnold, September 14, 1775, accessed at https://www.mountvernon.org/library/digitalhistory/quotes/article/every-post-is-honorable-in-which-a-man-can-serve-his-country/; page 24: Washington's Farewell Address, 1796, accessed at https://founders.archives.gov/documents/Washington/99-01-02-12223; page 26: "The Death of George Washington." *Digital Encyclopedia of George Washington*. Washington Library Center for Digital History, accessed at https://www.mountvernon.org/library/digitalhistory/digital-encyclopedia/article/the-death-of-george-washington/?cmp_id=258225311&adg_id=21928747871&kwd=george%20washington.

COVER: A portrait of President Washington

Table of Contents

CHAPTER 1

Meet George Washington

George Washington was the very first president of the United States. He is also known as one of America's Founding Fathers.

During the American Revolution, Washington led the Continental Army to victory. Later, he helped shape the U.S. Constitution. This important document sets up how our government should be run and lists citizens' basic rights. Perhaps most important, as president, he set the standard for how our country should be led.

George Washington had a reputation for honesty and bravery. He served the American people, in many roles, for more than 40 years. Today, many people consider Washington our country's greatest leader.

Washington was 57 years old when he took office as president.
"A good moral character is the first essential in a man."
—George Washington, December 5, 1790

This illustration shows young George Washington with his father.
When George was young, most wealthy families made sure their sons were well educated. However, George was self-taught. He had less schooling than the other Founding Fathers.

Country Boy from Virginia

George was born in Virginia on February 22, 1732. At the time, Virginia was one of the 13 British **colonies** in North America.

When George was just 11 years old, his father died. He left George a small piece of land and 10 **enslaved** people. George's older brothers had gone to school in England. But there wasn't enough money to send George.

George had always looked up to one of his older brothers, Lawrence. Now Lawrence became a father figure to George. He even introduced George to the man who would give him his first job, making maps.

This is an illustration of the house where Washington was born.

CHAPTER 2

Gaining Fame

In 1748, most Virginia colonists lived along the coast. But as people continued to arrive in North America, more land was needed. Washington went to **survey** Virginia's western frontier. Indigenous Peoples had been living there for thousands of years—and colonists were pushing them off the land. As a result, there was fighting between colonists and the Indigenous people.

In 1753, Washington returned to the frontier with a **militia** company. He tried to get the Indigenous people and their French allies to leave the land, but he was unsuccessful. In fact, his mission led to the French and Indian War. But tales of Washington's bravery made him famous.

Washington's surveying job gave him a chance to buy land. At that time, owning land was key to a person's success.
Every [job] is honorable in which a man can serve his country.
—George Washington, September 14, 1775

This illustration shows one artist's idea of George and Martha's wedding. In real life, Martha wore a yellow dress and no veil.

Like most other wealthy colonists, Martha and George ordered clothing, furniture, and other household items from England. For the most part, items like these were not manufactured in the colonies.

Gentleman Farmer

In 1759, Washington married Martha Dandridge Custis. She was a wealthy woman whose husband had died. Martha had two young children, whom Washington raised as his own.

Washington's brother Lawrence had died several years earlier. By 1761, Washington was the owner of Lawrence's estate, called Mount Vernon.

Washington used British agents to sell the tobacco he grew at Mount Vernon. He also relied on the agents to buy his goods from England. Washington felt he was being paid less for his crops than they were worth—and that the goods from England were overpriced. He realized the colonists needed to become financially independent of Great Britain.

Revolutionary Problem-Solver

The British taxed Americans to pay for fighting on the frontier. Many colonists thought the taxes were unfair because they had no say in British government.

The First Continental Congress began in September 1774. Representatives from every colony except Georgia met to discuss their British rulers. Washington was one representative from Virginia.

The colonists thought they could solve their problems peacefully. Then, on April 19, 1775, British soldiers fought with colonists at Lexington and Concord, in Massachusetts. It was the start of the American Revolution.

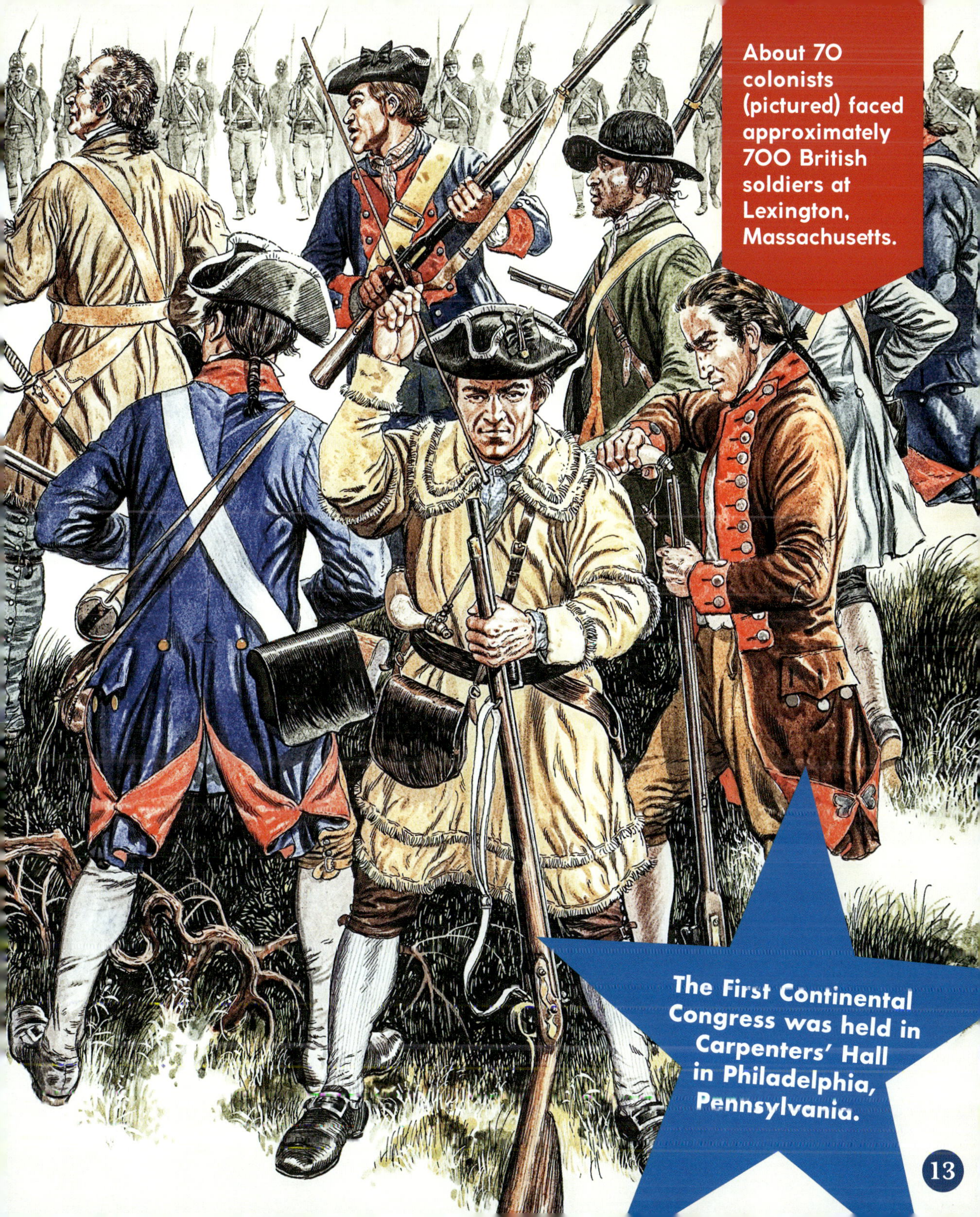
About 70 colonists (pictured) faced approximately 700 British soldiers at Lexington, Massachusetts.
The First Continental Congress was held in Carpenters' Hall in Philadelphia, Pennsylvania.

In December 1776, Washington crossed the Delaware River for a surprise attack on British forces in Trenton, New Jersey. The battle changed the course of the war.

Phillis Wheatley wrote a famous poem to celebrate Washington's leadership. She was born in Africa and enslaved in America. She was the first African American woman to publish a book.

14

Back in Command

The Second Continental Congress began in May. The decision was made to form a Continental Army. The men voted **unanimously** to make Washington its commander in chief.

Although Washington had never led an entire army, he accepted the position. He came up with battle plans and trained the army. For eight years, Washington led a group of tradesmen, farmers, and merchants against the greatest military power in the world: Great Britain. Many times it looked as if the cause was lost. But, in 1783, the colonists finally won their independence with help from the French.

Washington was chosen as president of the Constitutional Convention.
Rhode Island was the only state that didn't send a delegate to the convention.

A Fresh Start

America was now a free country. And Washington was a hero. Some thought he should be king. Washington disagreed. He returned to his work at Mount Vernon.

Then, in 1787, fifty-five men met in Philadelphia, Pennsylvania, to discuss the formation of a new government. The meeting became known as the Constitutional Convention.

Some of the men, like Washington, thought there should be a strong federal government. The states would be governed by one central authority, though each would have its own government, too. Others wanted individual state governments to have more power. It was not easy to come to an agreement. But eventually the men created the U.S. Constitution.

CHAPTER 4

Hello, Mr. President!

Washington had worked hard to get the Constitution approved by all the states. After that, he thought he'd return to work at Mount Vernon. But, once again, he was called to serve. The first presidential election was held in 1789. Though no one ran against him, Washington is known for being the first—and only—president to be elected by unanimous vote.

After being sworn into office on April 30, 1789, Washington moved into the presidential mansion. It was called the Franklin House or Osgood House. It was in New York City, which was the capital of the United States at the time. He set up the government and determined the roles and functions of the president.

This illustration shows President Washington being sworn into office.

It took Washington seven days to go from Mount Vernon to the ceremony in New York. In towns he passed through, people held parties and militias joined him.

Washington (far right) with his cabinet, from left to right: Knox, Jefferson, Randolph, and Hamilton.

Washington's cabinet was made up of four people. Today, the president's cabinet includes 15 or more people.

20

For the People

Washington knew that his actions would define the role of the president—and shape the entire government.

Washington chose his cabinet, which included four people. Thomas Jefferson was secretary of state. Alexander Hamilton was secretary of the treasury. Henry Knox was secretary of war. And Edmund Randolph was attorney general.

Washington also appointed judges to the U.S. Supreme Court, which is the highest court in the land. And he created a national bank to pay off the country's war debts. Washington even picked the spot where the permanent capital of the country would be. He chose a 100-square-mile area on the Potomac River. That area is today Washington, D.C.

Revolutionaries in France united around a saying that meant "Liberty, Equality, Brotherhood."
Washington's second inaugural address remains the shortest of any president's. It was only 135 words.

Round Two

In 1793, in another unanimous decision, Washington was elected for a second **term**. This time he focused more on the United States' relations with other countries. The French Revolution had begun in 1789. The French people rose up against their rulers. France later declared war against Great Britain and Spain.

Many people in America thought the United States should help the French. But Washington disagreed. He knew the country did not have the strength—or the money—to get involved in another war. He argued strongly that the United States should stay out of foreign affairs.

The Washington Monument In Washington, D.C. was dedicated in 1885.

After his second term, Washington looked forward to spending time at home with his family.

"Having now finished the work assigned me, I retire from the great theatre of Action."
—George Washington, December 23, 1783

Hard to Say Goodbye

Many people would have liked Washington to remain president forever. But Washington didn't want the presidency to be anything like the British government, where one person ruled until their death. He decided to step down after his second term. Like many things Washington did, this set the standard for future presidents. Even before it became a law, almost every president limited himself to two terms.

On September 19, 1796, Philadelphia's *American Daily Advertiser* published Washington's famous Farewell Address. It was delivered in the form of a public letter written to the American people.

Today about one million people visit Mount Vernon every year.

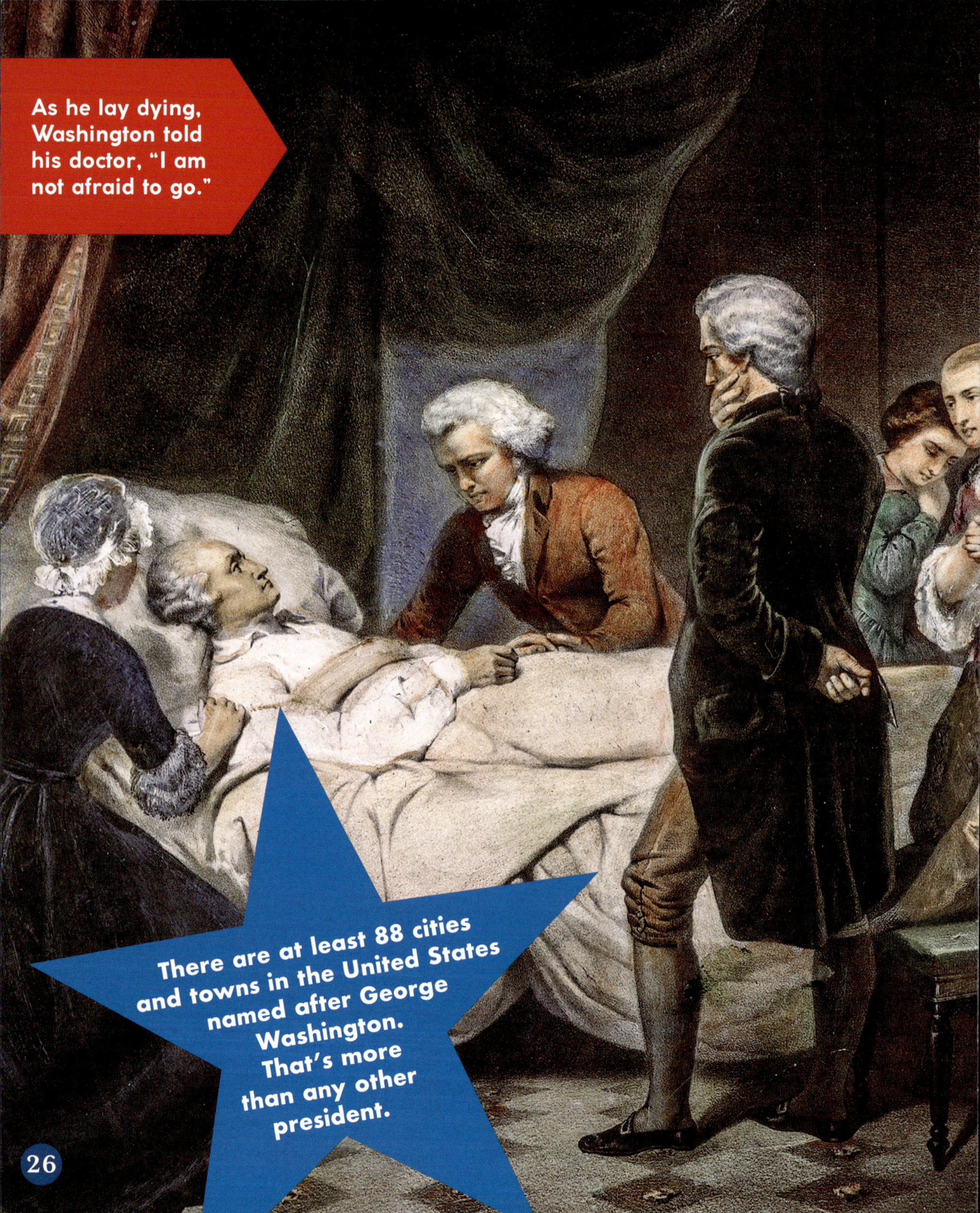

As he lay dying, Washington told his doctor, "I am not afraid to go."

There are at least 88 cities and towns in the United States named after George Washington. That's more than any other president.

A Life of Service

Washington did not get to enjoy his retirement for long. He died of a throat infection on December 14, 1799, at his home at Mount Vernon.

In his will, Washington said that the 123 enslaved people that belonged to him should be set free after his wife, Martha, died. Some people think his actions show that his views on slavery may have changed over the course of his life.

Becoming the president of a new and free nation was not an easy task. But George Washington was the right man for the job. Much of what we understand about how presidents should conduct themselves in office is based on the personality and character of the Father of Our Country: George Washington.

A New Government

In his first 100 days as president, and with the Constitution as his guide, Washington helped shape the new government into three branches. After the branches were formed, Washington filled their roles with men he knew could do the job.

Each branch plays a part in making sure that the government's power is balanced and that no one person or group always gets their way.

The president leads the branch of government

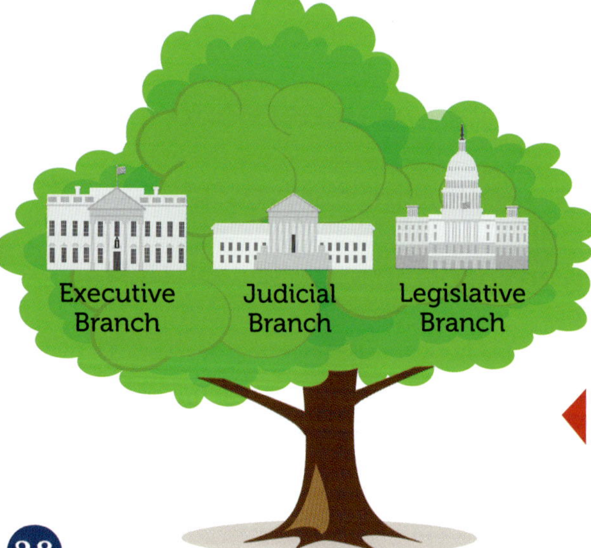

These are the three branches of our government.

called the executive branch. It also includes the vice president, the president's staff, and the cabinet. As the head of the executive branch, the president signs new bills into law.

Next is the judicial branch, which includes the Supreme Court. The Supreme Court is made up of justices who help apply the laws in the U.S.

Constitution to our lives as citizens.

Congress makes up the third branch, which is the legislative branch. It is divided into two parts: the House of Representatives and the Senate. Among other things, the people in Congress are responsible for writing new laws and declaring war.

American History

1744
King George's War, a struggle between Great Britain and France over territory in North America, begins in May. It lasts until 1748.

1754
The French and Indian War begins on July 3, when French soldiers attack Fort Necessity in an area that is now part of Pennsylvania.

1760
On October 25, George III becomes king of England. His policies eventually lead to the American Revolution.

| 1732 | 1744 | 1748 | 1754 | 1759 | 1760 |

George Washington's Life

1732
George Washington is born on February 22 in Westmoreland County, in the colony of Virginia.

1748
Washington accepts an offer to survey the Virginia frontier. The assignment gives Washington his first chance to become a landowner.

1759
George marries Martha Dandridge Custis on January 6. He raises her two children, "Jacky" and "Patsy," as his own.

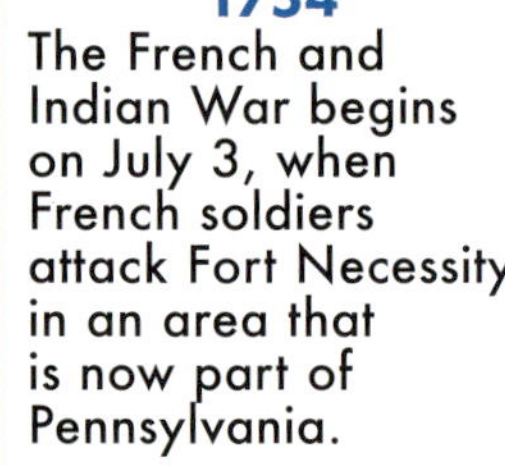

1775

On April 19, the first battle of the American Revolution takes place at Lexington and Concord in Massachusetts. The war officially ends eight years later, on September 3, 1783, with the Treaty of Paris. The United States officially becomes a country.

1787

The U.S. Constitution is accepted and signed on September 17. More than 200 years later, the Constitution is still the framework for our government and laws.

1808

The slave trade is officially outlawed in the United States, beginning January 1. But holding enslaved people is still legal.

| 1775 | 1787 | 1789 | 1799 | 1808 |

1775

Washington is chosen to be commander in chief of the Continental Army on June 19.

1789

On April 30, George Washington is sworn in as the first president of the United States. He serves two terms and is succeeded by John Adams.

1799

On December 14, Washington dies in his bed from a throat infection. He is 67 years old.

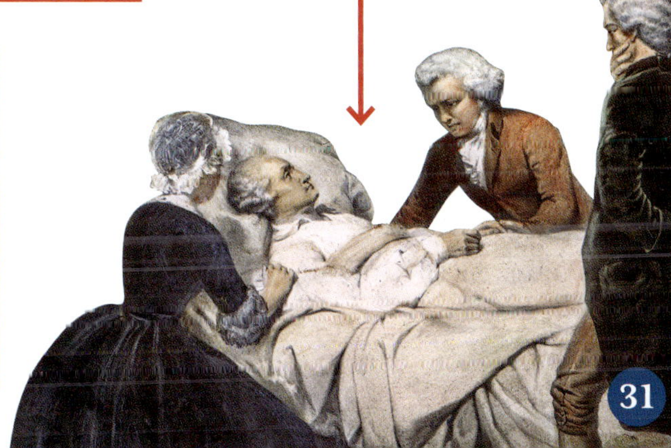

31

INDEX

ABOUT THE AUTHOR

Jevon Bolden is an editor and writer from sunny Florida. She has edited and written books for both kids and adults that teach them something new and help them experience the best in life. Jevon has a bachelor's degree in English from the University of Alabama.